!SAFETY CHECK!

EMERGENCIES

Written by
Valerie
Harvey

KidHaven
PUBLISHING

Published in 2027 by
KidHaven Publishing, an Imprint of Greenhaven Publishing, LLC
2544 Clinton St., Buffalo, NY 14224

Written by: Valerie Harvey
Edited by: Noah Leatherland
Designed by: Jasmine Pointer

Cataloging-in-Publication Data

Names: Harvey, Valerie.
Title: Emergencies / Valerie Harvey.
Description: Buffalo, NY : KidHaven Publishing, 2027. | Series: Safety check | Includes glossary and index.
Identifiers: ISBN 9781534570672 (pbk.) | ISBN 9781534570689 (library bound) | ISBN 9781534570696 (ebook)
Subjects: LCSH: Emergency management--Juvenile literature. | Public safety--Juvenile literature. | First responders--Juvenile literature.
Classification: LCC HV551.2 H378 2027 | DDC 363.348--dc23

Printed in the United States

CPSIA compliance information: Batch #CS27KH: For further information contact Greenhaven Publishing LLC at 1-844-317-7404.

Please visit our website, www.greenhavenpublishing.com.
For a free color catalog of all our high-quality books, call toll free 1-844-317-7404 or fax 1-844-317-7405.

Find us on

Image Credits
Cover - Hryshchyshen Serhii, Tanzeel Ur Rahman99. 4-5 - Golubovy, Wongsakorn 2468, Kitinut Jinapuck. 6-7 - FoxGrafy, RY_H, Elizaveta Galitckaia. 8-9 - Peakstock, PeopleImages, wavebreakmedia, Teerapong mahawan, John T Takai, Combotec, Fast_Cyclone, Gopal3366. 10-11 - MAYA LAB, thanmano, Apichet7579, Andrey_Popov. 12-13 - Brian A Jackson, Gorb Andrii, nik_nadal. 14-15 - Kzenon, arthierry, Chief Design, Inside Creative House. 16-17 - Andrew Angelov, O.PASH, The Studio, zo3listic. 18-19 - David Pereiras, Inamiqu, Ursula Page. 20-21 - Nadya So, PeopleImages, Technicsorn Stocker. 22-23 - Jihan Nafiaa Zahri, PreciousJ.

All images courtesy of Shutterstock.com, unless otherwise stated.

CONTENTS

Words that look like **this** can be found in the glossary on page 24.

WHAT IS AN EMERGENCY?

An emergency is a situation that people need to deal with quickly. It might be something such as a fire, someone getting hurt, or a pet in danger. Emergencies can feel scary, but knowing what to do if they happen makes a big difference.

You can stay calm, find a safe place, and ask a trusted adult for help. In this book, you'll learn how to recognize emergencies and how to respond safely and confidently!

STAYING CALM

When an emergency happens unexpectedly, it's easy to feel scared or worried. Take a deep breath, look around, and figure out what is safe to do. Moving carefully and speaking clearly to an adult can make a big difference.

Breathing deeply helps us stay calm.

Staying calm helps you think clearly and make smart choices. You can practice staying calm by having drills for different kinds of emergencies. You could even role-play this with your friends!

Practicing for emergencies helps you think through your options in different situations.

MEET THE EXPERTS

Emergency services are groups of people who are trained to help in all kinds of emergencies.

Paramedics care for and transport people who are hurt or feeling very sick.

Firefighters put out fires and rescue people from danger.

Police officers keep everyone safe and make sure rules are followed.

Lifeguards keep people safe at pools and beaches.

Knowing what these experts do can make it easier to ask for the right people's help in an emergency.

THE MAGIC NUMBER

When there is an emergency, it's important to get help quickly. You can call a special phone number to reach emergency services. You will be asked whether you need police, firefighters, or paramedics.

In the United States, you can call 911.

Different countries have their own emergency phone numbers. Ask a trusted adult to teach you the one for where you live. Practice what you should say, and make sure you know when it's the right time to call.

Only call the emergency number for a real emergency.

FIRE! FIRE!

If you see a fire inside a building, get out immediately—don't try to put it out yourself. Stay low to avoid smoke. Cover your nose and mouth with a cloth if you can and use the nearest safe exit.

Do not hide, go back inside, or try to carry things. Your safety comes first! Once you are outside, find a safe place and call the emergency number.

Fire drills help you remember exactly what to do if a fire happens.

WHEN SOMEBODY IS SICK OR INJURED

Sometimes, people might feel sick or get hurt. If this happens around you, stay calm and find an adult for help. If you can't find anyone and the person can't call the emergency number themselves, you can call the emergency number for help.

Only use the emergency phone number for serious situations.

While waiting, you can stay with the person and talk to them gently, but make sure that you stay safe yourself.

Knowing how to ask for help makes sure everyone gets the care they need quickly and safely.

WHAT IF I GET LOST?

Getting lost can feel scary, but there are ways to stay safe. If you can't find an adult you know, stay where you are and don't wander off. Try to stay close to where you last saw the adults you came with.

Look for a helper, such as a store worker or police officer, and tell them you're lost. Remembering your name, your address, and your parent or guardian's phone number can help you get back safely.

NATURAL EMERGENCIES

Natural disasters happen when nature causes sudden problems. These can include storms, floods, earthquakes, or strong winds. If a natural disaster happens, the most important thing is to stay safe.

Listen carefully to adults, and follow their instructions. They may tell you to move to a safer place or tell you to stay away from windows, water, or anything that could fall. Being prepared, knowing safe spots, and staying calm helps everyone stay safe during natural disasters.

DANGERS IN THE HOME

Even at home, some things can cause accidents if we're not careful. Hot stoves, sharp knives, cleaning products, and electrical outlets can all be dangerous. Things left on the floor could make people trip, and wet floors can be slippery.

The best way to stay safe is to ask an adult for help. Let them know if you see anything dangerous that needs to be moved out of the way. Knowing where the hazards are helps you enjoy your home safely without emergencies.

BE A SAFETY STAR

Being a Safety Star means knowing what to do when unexpected problems happen. You've learned how to stay calm, ask an adult for help, and call the emergency services if needed. You know how to stay safe around fires, injuries, natural disasters, and even when you get lost.

Can you be a Safety Star?

Practicing safe habits at home, outside, and with friends helps everyone. By paying attention, thinking clearly, and acting carefully, you can be a Safety Star every day!

GLOSSARY

fire drills practice runs of what to do if there is a fire

hazards things that could be dangerous or harmful

instructions steps that explain how to do something

role-play pretend to be someone else

INDEX